Sherlock Puzzle Book (Volume 1)

Unsolved Cases and Riddles Documented by Dr. John Watson

Mildred T. Walker

Get the full series with bonus contents on Amazon

Sherlock Puzzle Book (Volume 1-3):

Compilation Of 3 Books With Additional Bonus Contents By Mrs Hudson

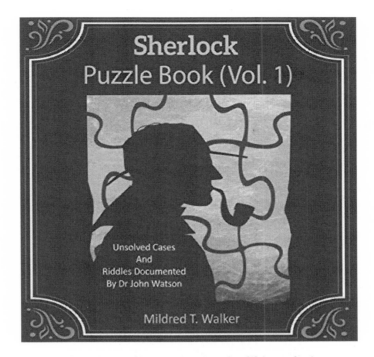

Get the audio version on Audible today!

Table of Contents

Table of Contents

Bluesource And Friends

Description

The Case of the Smoking Gun

The Case of The Mysterious Code

The Case of The Card Game

The Case of The Invisible Blade

The Case of The Killer Puzzle

The Case of The Club Repairs

The Case of The Mysterious Hanging

The Case of The Missing Sherlock

The Case of The Misdirected Snowball

The Case of The Missing Animals

The Case of The Horse Race

The Case of The Kidnapping

The Case of The Meeting Place

The Case of The Frosted Window

The Case of The Missing Birthday

The Case of The Two Thieves

The Case of The Missing Letters

The Case of The Cricket Club

The Case of The Circular House

The Case of The Missing Child

The Case of The Secret Message

The Case of The Killer First Day

The Case of The Trapped Detective

The Case of The Undead Husband

The Case of The Lonely Man

The Case of The Baggy Suit

The Case of The Sunday Murder

The Case of The Misplaced Wedding

The Case of The Mysterious Murderer

The Case of the Poisoned Tea

The Case of the Killer Pill

The Case of the Mysterious Windows

The Case of the Hidden Clues

The Case of the Bad Apple

The Case of the Murdered Captain

The Case of the Jumbled Notes

The Case of the Mixed-up Witnesses

The Case of the Thwarted Highwayman

The Case of the Escaped Stalker

The Case of the Frozen Hermit

The Case of the Servant's Wish

The Case of the Funny Mirror

The Case of the Wise Son

The Case of the Missing Gold

The Case of the Broken Watch

The Case of the Grimm Reaper

The Case of the Surprise Ending

(Bonus Case)

Answers

(Answers) The Case of the Smoking Gun

(Answers) The Case of the Mysterious Code

(Answers) The Case of the Card Game

(Answers) The Case of the Invisible Blade

(Answers) The Case of the Killer Puzzle

(Answers) The Case of the Club Repairs

(Answers) The Case of the Mysterious Hanging

(Answers) The Case of the Missing Sherlock

(Answers) The Case of the Misdirected Snowball

(Answers) The Case of the Missing Animals

(Answers) The Case of the Horse Race

(Answers) The Case of the Kidnapping

(Answers) The Case of the Meeting Place

(Answers) The Case of the Frosted Window

(Answers) The Case of the Missing Birthday

(Answers) The Case of the Two Thieves

(Answers) The Case of the Missing Letters

(Answers) The Case of the Cricket Club

(Answers) The Case of the Circular House

(Answers) The Case of the Missing Child

(Answers) The Case of the Secret Message

(Answers) The Case of the Killer First Day

(Answers) The Case of the Trapped Detectives

(Answers) The Case of the Undead Husband

(Answers) The Case of the Lonely Man

(Answers) The Case of the Baggy Suit

(Answers) The Case of the Sunday Murder

(Answers) The Case of the Misplaced Wedding

(Answers) The Case of the Mysterious Murderer

(Answers) The Case of the Poisoned Tea

(Answers) The Case of the Killer Pill

(Answers) The Case of the Mysterious Window

(Answers) The Case of the Hidden Clues

(Answers) The Case of the Bad Apple

(Answers) The Case of the Murdered Captain

(Answers) The Case of the Jumbled Notes

(Answers) The Case of the Mixed-up Witnesses

(Answers) The Case of the Thwarted Highwayman

(Answers) The Case of the Escaped Stalker

(Answers) The Case of the Frozen Hermit

(Answers) The Case of the Servant's Wish

(Answers) The Case of the Funny Mirror

(Answers) The Case of the Wise Son

(Answers) The Case of the Hidden Gold

(Answers) The Case of the Broken Watch

(Answers) The Case of the Grimm Reaper

(Answers) The Case of the Surprise Ending

Conclusion

liable for any hardship or damages that may befall them after undertaking information described herein.

Additionally, the information in the following pages is intended only for informational purposes and should thus be thought of as universal. As befitting its nature, it is presented without assurance regarding its prolonged validity or interim quality. Trademarks that are mentioned are done without written consent and can in no way be considered an endorsement from the trademark holder.

Bluesource And Friends

This is book is brought to you by Bluesource And Friends, a happy book publishing company.

Our motto **"Happiness Within Pages"**

We promise to deliver amazing value to readers with our books.

We also appreciate honest book reviews from our readers.

Connect with us on our Facebook page www.facebook.com/bluesourceandfriends and stay tuned to our latest book promotions and free giveaways.

Introduction

My companion and dear friend Mr. Sherlock Holmes
has become a familiar name to all. Indeed, it would
seem that his name is splashed across the front page
of the newspaper every week. Anybody with a
penchant for criminal investigation knows who he is.
His fame is justly deserved. In my opinion, there is no
other person with his skills and abilities.

I have been so fortunate to work with Mr. Holmes on
many occasions. Though my skills are not as good as
his, I will do my best to chronicle his work. For many
years, we have shared quarters in 221B Baker Street
and I would like to believe that this time has enriched
both of our lives. I am John Watson, a doctor by
profession.

Mr. Holmes has long dreamed of improving the
minds of others. He has spoken about creating a book
that would instill habits that are believed to be vital in
the art of deduction. This would be a revolutionary
step in humanity and would certainly address critical
thinking, mathematical and scientific knowledge, and
logical analysis. Alas, this has yet to happen.

No matter how much work calls him away, Mr.
Holmes has never given up in improving my modest
faculties. He had given me innumerable occasions to
engage my mind and solve a riddle, which to him is

already clear. These have been quite taxing at times, but I engage in each one to the best of my abilities. To not do so would be to dishonor the ability he is sharing with me to improve my analytical ability.

In truth, I do believe it has helped. I am more aware than I was in my youth. I am less apt for hasty conclusions. If I have gained expertise in these areas, it is all due to my dear friend. Show me a sickly patient, and I can confidently present you with a diagnosis. I will then, to the limits of medical science, provide them with a recovery. But my mind does not work naturally with deception and criminality. In a perfect world, we would coexist in honor. Alas, this is not the case. Mr. Holmes is better equipped for the undertow of the real world.

For those who are constantly exposed to such matters, the results are powerful. Thus, I have decided to assemble a collection. Working through my notes, I have compiled cases that Mr. Holmes and I have been presented with. I have described the moments as I first encountered them, with all the pertinent information provided. The answers provide all of the useful details. Some are my own answers that I reached myself, Others are Holmes' explanations.

It is my hope that you find these cases as intriguing as Mr. Holmes and I did. If they might prove to sharpen your deductive reasoning just a little, it would give me all the vindication that I need. The credit, though, must go to Holmes. As always, I am content in being only the scribe. Every effort has been made to ensure that every problem has a fair solution. But, if by happenstance you should find that not to be the case, the blame should fall to me. None should fall on my dear friend, Mr. Holmes.

My beloved friends, it is my pleasure to share with you these unsolved cases of Sherlock Holmes.

Dr. John Watson

Cases

The Case of the Smoking Gun

Mr. Holmes and I were interrupted one summer afternoon by Mrs. Hudson. She informed us that our presence was requested at the scene of a murder. Mr. Holmes and I arrived to find the police gathered around a body. Four men stood off to the side. While a gun laid at the feet of the deceased man.

I followed as Holmes walked up to one of the officers.

"What has happened?" Sherlock asked.

"One of those four men have killed this young man."

The officer commenced his recounting of what the four men had told him.

Frank played a game of rugby with one of the innocent men the day before.

Leopold had considered becoming a farmer before he moved to the city.

Edward, an excellent printer, was planning on teaching Joseph how to use the new lithograph.

The murderer had undergone amputation surgery on his leg last month.

Joseph had only been introduced to Theodore six months ago.

Theodore had hidden away after the murder took place until the police arrived.

Frank used to be a heavy drinker.

Joseph and Edward had built their lithographs together.

Theodore's brother is the murderer. They grew up in London together.

Sherlock immediately turned to face me, a smile across his face.

"My dear Watson, I know who the murderer is."

Who is the murderer?

The Case of The Mysterious Code

I watched as Holmes paced the length of the cold office. The sun had dipped under the horizon long ago, but alas, we were still here. We had received the call about the murder early, but it had thus far been a quizzical one.

Pranay Patel had been found dead at his desk by his secretary, Jason Kumar.

Holmes and I had questioned several people, but none of them seemed to be the murderer.

"I believe I have narrowed down the suspect to three people," Holmes announced.

"Which three?" I asked.

"The secretary, Jason Kumar; his wife, Keya; and his friend, Mr. Gupta."

The three suspects had visited Mr. Patel at some point on the day of his murder.

They had given Holmes their reasoning, but for the life of me, I could not figure out how that had given him enough information to know one of the three had to be the murderer.

"Why those three?" I enquired.

"Look over here, dear Watson."

I stepped over to where Holmes stood. In the corner of the room where Mr. Patel's office desk stood, I searched the blank wall for what Holmes was pointing at. Subsequently, I saw what he had found.

"It appears to be a series of nonsense numbers and letter."

"No, Watson, it is not," Sherlock stated, irritated, "That is the murderer."

"How does 7B91011 tell you who the murderer is?"

"You tell me."

Who is the killer?

The Case of The Card Game

One dreary spring day, Holmes and I sat watching the rain splash on the window.

Mrs. Hudson had raced through the flat early that morning, telling Holmes he needed to clean. Holmes, as he so often did, said he would do it later. Before leaving, she invited us to a bridge game, but Holmes did not accept.

"I do wish someone would call," Holmes declared, lighting his pipe.

I glanced to my left and spied a deck of cards. Today was my day to stump my dear friend. "I have something to help us pass the time," I stated.

Holmes glanced up over his pipe at me. He stared at me incredulously. His ideas for pastime were much different than my own but I was certain that he would enjoy what I had planned.

"What is your idea?" he asked, sending another blue plume of smoke up from his pipe. I reached over for the deck of cards and opened the box. I shuffled the cards between my hands, I picked out four and laid them face down in front of Holmes.

"I have a puzzle for you," I declared.

"You do? With those cards?"

"With these four."

"Out of a deck of 52 cards, you plan to stump me with only four. I am piqued by the exclamation."

I smiled slightly at my dear friend. It wasn't often that I could present him with a puzzle like this. I was normally the one getting stumped by Holmes' queries.

"My dear friend, there is a bit of information that I must share with you. The left card can't be higher than the card on the right. The difference between card one and card three equals eight. None of these cards are Aces. There are no face cards. The difference between card two and card four is seven. What are the four cards?"

Holmes thought for a moment before smiling.

What are the numbers on the cards?

$$\begin{array}{cccc} 2 & 3 & 10 & 10 \\ \underline{2} & \underline{2} & \underline{10} & \underline{9} \\ 1 & 2 & 3 & 4 \end{array}$$

$$1 \leftrightarrow 3 = 8 \qquad 2 \to 4 = 7$$

$$1 \leq 4$$

The Case of The Invisible Blade

Holmes and I stepped into the cold sitting room of a small flat. A young man laid on the floor in front of the mirror in a semi-naked state.

An officer walked over to Holmes and me. A perplexed look covered his face.

"When the decedent was found, the room had been closed from the inside. We have not found any signs of an intruder. The windows and doors were all locked and nothing was broken. We found no signs of a struggle either," the officer began.

Holmes stepped closer to the body. A large pool of blood had gathered under the young man.

"Are there any wounds?" I asked the officer.

Blood of this amount indicated that there was a large wound. I could not see such a wound that would constitute the amount of blood.

"We have searched the body, but we could not find any incisions."

Holmes knelt beside the body and inspected the pants. The pants had been lying on the floor with the belt still around them.

"You have not come to any conclusions," Holmes stated.

"No, sir, we have not," the officer replied.

"Watson?"

"The young man had to be stabbed, but how and with what, I could not say. If no incisions were found, then I am baffled at what has happened."

"I know what happened."

How was this man murdered?

The Case of The Killer Puzzle

The summer sun beat down on Holmes and me as we walked up to a small country cottage. We received the call earlier of the murder of a woman. One of the officers stepped out of the cottage and greeted us.

"We have the suspects inside if you would like to speak with them," the officer offered.

Holmes nodded his head and stepped inside. The victim, a young woman, laid across the couch. Three women stood off to the side, their eyes downcast.

"Are those women the only suspects?" I asked.

"Yes," the officer replied, "They were the only three who were present at the scene."

Holmes stepped up to the women, lighting a cigarette and puffing a plume of smoke over their heads.

"Please introduce yourselves," he stated.

"I am Alice. I am... was her friend. We were going out tonight."

"I am Debra. I came with Alice."

"I am Sia, the maid."

Holmes turned back to the victim. A small square of paper poked out of her hands. Holmes reached out and took the square of paper. He handed the paper to me. On it was written, *"2ⁿᵈ of January, 3ʳᵈ of July, 4ᵗʰ of April, 2ⁿᵈ of October, 4ᵗʰ of December."*

"Do you know what this means?" I asked.

"It's the killer. Do you know what it says?"

I thought for a moment, reading over the note again.

"I do."

Who's the killer?

The Case of The Club Repairs

"I have a conundrum for you, Watson," Holmes declared, cutting the silence of our lazy afternoon.

I laid down the book that I had been reading and turned to look at my glassy-eyed friend. He had just returned from a meeting with his Criminologist Club.

Those meetings normally meant that I would be presented with a question or two.

"What happened tonight?" I asked.

"The Treasurer of the club called the meeting tonight. We have a few repairs that need to be made in our meeting place. We were meeting to discuss how much the repairs would cost and who would pay for them."

"It wasn't your regular meeting, I see."

"Alas, not nearly as fun, but it does make for a wonderful mathematical problem. Do you feel ready?"

"I suppose. My brain could use a good stretch."

"The treasurer informed us that the repairs would cost $2040. We all agreed that we would split the payment equal among all of the members. Unfortunately, four of our members decided to resign. This meant that we each had to pay an extra $17. How many members were originally in our club?"

How many members were originally in the Criminologists'
Club?

The Case of The Mysterious Hanging

Lightning flashed outside and illuminated the sitting room.

Holmes and I had been enjoying a sabbatical of sorts. It seemed as the never-ending rain had kept murder at bay.

That soon ended. A quick succession of raps came from the door.

"Watson, do you mind?" Holmes asked, gritting over his pipe.

With a sigh, I stood and went to the door. The door opened with a creak. A Scotland Yard officer stood on the other side of the door.

"Is Mr. Holmes in?" the officer asked.

"He is. Won't you come in?"

The officer stepped inside and reached a hand out to Holmes. Holmes grasped his hand with a firm shake.

"I was hoping I would find you here. We have a case we need you to look at. None of the officers have been able to figure out what happened."

"I suppose our sabbatical is over, Watson."

Holmes and I dressed in our Mackintosh and followed the officer down the street. Officers strolled around the perimeter of the building.

The first thing I noticed about this home was that there were no windows. A lone door provided the only access to the room inside.

Once inside, we saw that the room was completely empty. There were no tables or seats. The only thing in the room was a large puddle of water just under an empty rope.

"We've already removed the body, but we haven't figured out how she got herself up there."

"You're certain that nobody did this to her?" I asked.

"The only door was locked when we arrived. We had to knock it down to get inside."

"How long had she been hanging?" Sherlock asked.

"Her neighbor hadn't seen her for a week before she contacted us."

"Hmm."

Holmes walked over to the puddle of water and looked up at the ceiling.

I had a sneaking suspicion that he already knew what had happened. I knew what happened as well.

Wanting to impress my friend, I spoke first.

How did the woman hang herself?

The Case of The Missing Sherlock

Sherlock had been on the cusp of uncovering a smuggled ring when he went missing. I hadn't heard from him in the three days.

I had spent the last three days scouring every inch of the flat and all of his known locations trying to find any clue as to his whereabouts. Mrs. Hudson had even seemed worried.

This particular Sunday, she dropped in to see if he had returned.

"Have you heard from him?" Mrs. Hudson asked.

"No, I'm afraid. I've got one last place to search. It's the last place I know that he has been."

"I do hope the poor dear is alright. It's so unlike him to not check in."

"I was supposed to go with him on his last outing, but he left before I returned home."

"Did he say anything?"

"The same thing he always says, 'If I go missing, look in the last place.'"

"He never speaks plain English, does he?"

"He seems not."

Mrs. Hudson ran a finger along the mantle of the fireplace, a normal habit of hers. While she may have been worried about Holmes, her landlady insight was still intact.

"One thing I can say, this place has never been cleaner, or quieter."

This had been very quiet, but I had to get Mrs. Hudson to leave. I had to get down to the last place before it was too late. I was certain that Holmes had left a clue for me there.

"Mrs. Hudson, I know you're concerned, but I will contact you as soon as I hear something from him. But I must leave. I only have a small window of time to inspect the last place."

"Alright, I shouldn't have kept you this long. I must get home to fix Mr. Hudson's meal."
I was concerned about Holmes, but I was equally concerned about poor Mr. Hudson. Food like Mrs. Hudson's shouldn't be fed to pigs.

I slipped into my frock and made my way out onto the cold winter streets of London. Checking behind me to make sure I wasn't being followed, I slipped down an alley and to the door of the last known location of Holmes.

The door opened into a dark damp room with a single light. Just as I had figured, I should have started here. On the table was a note from Holmes.

When we spoke last, Holmes had informed me that he had narrowed down his suspects to three people: Joseph, Bill, and John.

31

Reaching out to take the note off the table, I quickly realized that Holmes had written his message in code.

The paper read: 710 57735 34 5508 51 7718. It had to be the name of the suspect who could lead me to Holmes' location.

Who is the criminal?

The Case of The Misdirected Snowball

One snowy night, Holmes and I sat at home by the fire, warming ourselves. It had been quite the day, but it was sure to be a calm night.

I rolled a cigarette as Holmes lit his pipe. Silence filled the room as I drifted to sleep. Before slumber took over, I was shaken awake by a crash.

Holmes and I jumped from our seats to investigate.

At the far side of the room, a snowball had broken through the window. Through the window we watched three young brothers run down the street. The brothers were John, Mark, and Paul Crimson.

"We need to get this glass cleaned up before somebody gets hurt," I said. "Yes… We do."

Holmes wasn't paying attention to the glass or the window; he was still watching the boys. I retrieved a broom and swept up the glass before he stepped back.

"I need to talk with those boys," Holmes said.

"You don't know which one did this. They probably didn't mean to."

"They must learn to take responsibility for the things they do, accident or not."

"Let's get some sleep. You can pay them a visit tomorrow."

Holmes begrudgingly trudged to his room. I covered the broken window, making a mental note to let Mrs. Hudson know what had transpired.

The next morning, I woke to the sound of tapping on the door. Holmes answered the door, finding nobody but a note fixed on the door.

"What does it say?" I asked.

Holmes showed me the paper. On it was written, "? Crimson. He broke your window."

"What does it mean?" I asked.

"I know who I need to speak with about my window."

Which brother broke the window?

The Case of The Missing Animals

The most peculiar day started with the most peculiar request for Holmes and me.

A young boy paid us a visit and asked us to accompany him back to his father's farm. It seemed that three of their animals had been stolen.

"I don't typically do work like this," Holmes said.

"Please," the young boy pleaded, "My father needs those animals back, and we have the three men who had to have done it."

"Holmes, this should only take a few minutes out of our day. We have nothing else going on."

Holmes sighed. He waved a hand towards the door and the boy led the way out of the flat. After a long ride out to the farm, Holmes and I were met by an old man and three young men.

"You came," the old man exclaimed.

"Yes, well, my day has been slow. I haven't got a lot of time, so please, point in the direction of the criminals."

The old man nodded and turned to the three young men, pointing at each one in turn.

"These are the men that stole my animals; a cat, a dog, and a hen."

"What do you need help with if you know they stole the animals?" I asked.

"They each stole one, but we don't know who stole which one."

"Names?" Holmes asked.

The old man pointed at each, naming them off, "Robin, Steve, and Tim."

"Robin, what do you have to say?" Holmes asked.

"Tim stole the hen."

"Steve?"

"Tim stole the dog."

"Tim?"

"Both are lying. I stole neither the dog nor the hen."

"Watson, the man who stole the cat is lying, but the one who stole the hen is
telling the truth. Who stole which animal?"

Who stole which animal?

The Case of The Horse Race

Holmes had left the flat early one spring morning. I had spent the day cleaning; something that Holmes never took the time to do.

Shortly before nightfall, Holmes came through the door.

"Watson, I have a conundrum for you."

He must have had a wonderful day. Only when something interesting happens did he come home with a conundrum for me.

The day had been a rather lazy one, so something to work my brain sounded nice.

"What is it?" I asked.

"I just spent the day at the horse races. The first race was the best. There were five horses in total: Dusky, Peanuts, Park, Classic, and Royal. Park crossed the finish line before Peanuts, but after Royal. Dusky was able to cross the finish line before Classic but after Peanuts. Now, tell me the order in which they finished the race?"

Holmes sat across from me and studied the book I had been reading. This was one of the simpler quizzes he had presented me.

What order did the horses finish the race?

The Case of The Kidnapping

Over the past month, Holmes had been rather beside himself. His old enemy, Professor Moriarty, had started his old games again.

Every other day, he had kidnapped a prominent member in London. He was holding them for ransom, but as of yet, had not received any money.

Holmes and I had been working to track down Moriarty, but he was always a couple of steps ahead.

Holmes paced by the fireplace, his pipe in hand. I hadn't seen him this distraught since the last time Moriarty made an appearance.

"I must find out who he plans on taking next," Holmes mumbled to himself.

"Sit down," I stated, "You will solve nothing if you wear yourself down pacing."

Just as Holmes reached for a chair, a knock sounded from the door. Holmes flashed away. In a trice, he was back with a note in his hand.

"Who was that?" I asked.

"A young boy with a message from a man he identified as Mr. M."

"What does the note say?"

"It's a series of numbers, 603 60432."

"Do you know what it means?"

Holmes looked across the room at the mirror. A light flashed across his eyes.

"Yes, I know what this means. It's the next target."

Who is the next target for Moriarty?

The Case of The Meeting Place

The cool evening air blew through the sitting room where I waited to receive word from Holmes.

He had told me not to plan anything, that we were going to be busy. I had spent the majority of the afternoon reading and waiting for him to return home.

It was drawing close to night, and still no word. A knock sounded from the door.

A young lad, Jason, stood at the door with a note in his hand. Holmes often used Jason to deliver messages.

If memory serves me correctly, all of his messages were always in code.

I took the note from Jason and handed him three pence. Glancing at the note, I saw a series of numbers, 5 14 9 7 13 1 2 1 11 5 18 19 20 18 5 5 20.

What location is the meeting place?

The Case of The Frosted Window

One wintry evening as Holmes and I ambled around the house doing nothing of particular importance, a knock came from the door. Holmes, who stood the closest to the door, said, "Watson, would you please?"

I didn't question his request; he was likely deep in thought so much so that answering the door would have ripped him from the process.

The door squeaked open to reveal a police officer standing with an old man. The man was dressed as a servant, and by the look on his face, he had a story to tell.

"Good afternoon. Who do we have here?"

"This is Wilfred; he has requested to speak with Mr. Holmes on a personal matter."

"Personal?"

"The lady of the house has been murdered, and he wants Holmes to help solve the case.

We feel we have it pretty well wrapped up."

"I see. Well, come in then. You can catch your death of cold out there."

The officer and Wilfred stepped inside and dusted the snow off their shoulders. Holmes faced away from them, thinking about something.

"Sherlock, you have guests," I said, catching his eye.

"Ah, I suppose I will get back to what I was thinking about later. What do you need?"

"I am the servant of Annie Barnes. I found her dead this afternoon."

"I see, and you don't trust Scotland Yard to find the killer."

"No, sir, I do not."

"Then please, tell me what transpired."

"Yes sir. I was finishing my work I noticed that her study light was on. I had stoked up the fire in her office a while earlier, but she had said she wouldn't be in the office much longer. Frost had formed on the window, so I wiped it away to look inside. I saw her, then, slumped over the desk. I immediately kicked in the door and found that she was dead. I immediately called the police."

Holmes stared out the far window. Something was off about this man's story and Holmes knew it as well.

"I'm surprised you would come to me for help. You should have known that I would catch you right off the bat," Holmes said.

"What do you mean?" Wilfred asked.

"You killed the lady."

"How do you know that?" the officer inquired.

How did Sherlock know Wilfred killed Annie?

The Case of The Missing Birthday

One winter evening, Holmes and I sat watching the snow fall outside as we warmed ourselves next to the fire.

It was the first of a New Year, and Holmes and I enjoyed the holidays with minimal interruptions.

I picked up the newspaper and read through some of the front pages before something struck my mind.

"Holmes, when is your birthday?"

"You guess, my dear Watson."

If I had known, I wouldn't have asked him. Alas, Holmes saw this as a learning experience for me.

In all my life with Holmes, I couldn't remember him mentioning a birthday. I knew we hadn't celebrated one.

"I have no idea," I stated.

"I will tell you this. Two days ago, I was 40 and next year I will turn 43."

"That's not possible."

Holmes grinned around his pipe and turned his attention back to his book.

He wasn't going to let me in on the secret. I had to figure it out for myself.

What day of the year is Holmes' birthday?

The Case of The Two Thieves

Holmes and I had been working on a case involving two thieves.

They had done a very good job at covering their tracks, but they hadn't been smart enough to outsmart Holmes.

We seemed to be a couple of steps behind them, but we still hadn't figured out where they were headed next.

"Do we have any new information?" I asked Holmes as he looked through some papers on the men.

"The only information I have to gather thus far is that they were born on the same day, in the same year, to the same parents."

"Why, that must mean that they are twins."

"No, they aren't twins."

"Why, that's not possible. They must be if they were born on the same day and year, and to the same mother."

Holmes didn't respond. He continued to look through the papers in his hands.

Somehow, he was right. Two men had been born on the same day and year to the same mother, yet they were not twins.

How could the men not be twins?

47

The Case of The Missing Letters

Holmes and I were having dinner one summer evening.

I sat working on a case that I had recently acquired.

I wanted to do my best and prove to myself and Holmes that I was just as talented as he was.

Alas, I found myself confused and befuddled quite often.

I found a sheet of paper with a clue on it that I was certain would help me crack the case, but I couldn't figure out the last of the sequence.

Two letters had been torn off the paper before I received it. All that was written on it was JFMAMJJASO.

With a sigh, I slid the paper over to Holmes to ask him for help.

"I have tried the entire day to figure out the last two letters of this sequence," I said.

"Would you like me to tell you what they are?" Holmes replied.

"You already know?"

"Yes, it's quite simple."

What are the last two letters in the sequence JFMAMJJASO?

The Case of The Cricket Club

The summer sun had begun to disappear as Holmes and I stepped inside of the Cricket Clubhouse.

Scotland Yard had asked us to come and help find the suspect of the crime.

Five men, the suspects, stood off to the side. Each one was accompanied by an officer.

The men were, John Albers, Jim Davis, Marty Brown, Tom Stevenson, and Bob Edison.

"How much work have the officers performed?" I asked Holmes.

"I don't know."

One of the other officers stepped forward, a notepad in hand.

"Holmes and Watson, I presume."

"Yes," Holmes replied.

"We have spoken with the suspects, witnesses, and others who know the suspects and have gathered a lot of information. We still haven't been able to narrow down who the suspect is."

The officer shared the information they had gathered as I quickly jotted down the information in my journal.

None of the suspects had the same color of shoes, wife's first name, height, weight, or hair color.

The red-haired suspect weighed 140 pounds.

Bob Edison stood 5 feet 3 inches tall.

The culprit's wife was Mary.

The suspect who weighs 150 pounds doesn't stand 5 feet 9 inches tall.

One suspect's wife's name is Pam, but he does not have blonde hair.

Jim Davis' shoes are colored orange.

John Albert's hair is black.
One suspect's wife's name is Betty, and he weighs 200 pounds.

Tom Stevenson weighs 210 pounds.

The suspect who is 200 pounds doesn't have any hair.

The suspect who is married to Cathy also weighs 140 pounds.

Mary Brown's hair is brown.

The suspect with black hair is married to Mary.

The suspect who is bald is not wearing orange colored shoes.

Holmes looked over at me as I wrote down the last of the information. He had a sly grin on his face.

He had already figured out who had committed the crime, but he wasn't going to share his discovery just yet.

Who committed the crime?

The Case of The Circular House

Holmes and I walked to the circular house that loomed in front of us.

It was the dead of the night, but the parents had returned home to find their children murdered.

"Thank you for coming," the mother cried, ferociously shaking Holmes' hand.

"We phoned the police, but we wanted to have the best detective here as well," the father added.

"It's our job to help in times like these. Please tell us what happened," Holmes stated.

"My wife and I were going to a party tonight. Before we left, we tucked our younger children into bed and kissed them goodnight. The older children were still up, but we kissed them goodnight before we left, as well. When we returned, the children were dead."

"Is there anything more that you can tell us?" I asked.

"Yes, actually," the mother began. "The gardener, the butler, and the maid were here with the children. The butler was feeding the older children, the gardener had been watering the plants, and the maid was dusting the corners."

"Peculiar," Holmes said, turning to the house.

I followed Holmes' gaze. The officer who had fetched us has said the maid, butler, and gardener had told him the same thing the mother had told us.

One of them had to be the killer, but which one. I had a sneaking suspicion who it was, and I knew Holmes knew.

Who is the killer?

The Case of The Missing Child

The air in the garden cooled in the evening light.

Holmes and I sat enjoying a pot of tea when a young boy ran up to us. His breath came in shutters. It looked as if he had run a long way.

"The lady needs your help," the young boy huffed.

"What has happened?" I asked.

"The lady came home and found her son had been kidnapped. Please, Mr. Holmes, she needs you to find her son."

Holmes sat his pipe down and stood.

"Lead the way," Holmes said.

Holmes and I followed the boy down the street and up to a magnificent home.

The lady was an affluent member of the town. Thus, the child was taken as a means to get something from her for his return.

The lady looked up as we walked up the steps in the back garden.

"I'm glad you could make it," she said through her tears.

"Please, tell us what happened."

The lady informed us that she had left to have tea
with her friends and left her eight-year-old son in the
care of her servants and her sheepdog, Sir Foo Foo.

Her servants included:
Dorothy the dentist,
Lawrence the lawyer,
Devon the doctor,
McKenzie the music instructor,
Sadie the seamstress,
Lucy the launderer,
Joel the jester,
Constantine the carpenter,
Anastasia the accountant,
Sandy the sweeper,
Bernadette the barber,
Geraldo the groundskeeper,
Boris the butler,
Magdalena the maid,
Philip the photographer,
Tiffany the tutor,
Griffith the gardener,
and Surlamina the Secretary of State.

The lady had taken it upon herself to speak with each
of her servants to try and figure out which one had
taken her son. She received the following alibis from
them:
Harold was exercising,
Griffith was in the garden planting roses,
Tiffany was going over the boy's homework,
Philip was photographing the garden,
Magdalena was making the beds,
Boris was cleaning the stairs,
Geraldo was watching Griffith work,
Bernadette was tending to Sir Foo Foo,
Sandy was sweeping,

Anastasia was taking care of the affairs of the Lady,
Constantine was building a birdhouse,
Joel was working on his jokes,
Lucky was taking care of the laundry,
Sadie was making a new dress for the Lady,
McKenzie was practicing the flute,
Lawrence was suing the bank,
Dorothy was looking at the Lady's dental information,
Devon was looking of the medical charts of the Lady,
and Surlamina was being the Secretary of State.

Once the Lady finished her statement, Holmes
declared, "There is only one possible kidnapper."

Who kidnapped the child?

The Case of The Secret Message

I sat in the sitting room with a cigarette in hand,
staring at the front door.

It had been eight hours since Holmes had left.

He had told me he would send a messenger with his
location in four hours. He had left me with a list of
words, which I could only assume was his code.

At the top of the list of words read: "I can only use
these words in the happenchance that my message is
intercepted:
Zebra,
Legend,
Yolk,
You,
Beam,
Train,
Soldier,
Fruits,
None,
Chemic,
Box,
Rear,
Quiz,
Psycho,
Coins,
Pizza,
One,
Kept,
Lazy,
Technique,
Keen,
Eleven,

Walk."

I had not yet figured out what those words could
mean, but once I received his message, I was certain I
would discover their meaning.

A quiet knock sounded from the door. I rushed
forwards and opened the door to discover a small lad
holding a note.

Offering him five pence, I took the note.

As I unfolded the paper, I discovered that the note
made as much sense as the list of words.

On it read:
"Fruits Psycho Rear Technique Soldier Kept
Rear Psycho Walk
Eleven Zebra Soldier Kept
Soldier You Soldier Coins Eleven Box."

Where is Holmes?

The Case of The Killer First Day

Holmes and I walked up the steps to the front of the schoolhouse.

It has been a long while since I had walked these steps.

Receiving a call from a school was a bit unheard of for Holmes and me.

Alas, there was a murder that needed to be solved.

The unfortunate soul was a young boy, Jacob. What's worse, it was the very first day of school. An officer approached Holmes and me as we stepped into the sunlit hallway.

"We have the four teachers we believe to be the main suspects," the officer informed us.

"Who do we have?" Holmes asked.

The officer introduced us to the four suspects.

The first was Alice, who claimed to be reading the newspaper at the time of the murder.

The second was Elizabeth, who said she was checking the chemistry papers.

The third was Sara, who said she had locked herself in her room.

The fourth was Clair, who claimed she was getting ready for orientation.

Holmes looked at each of the school teachers in turn. He looked at me, a glimmer in his eye.

"I know who the killer is," Holmes pronounced.

Who's the killer?

The Case of The Trapped Detective

Holmes and I had found ourselves in quite a predicament.

Moriarty and his ever-scheming mind had trapped us in a dirt floor cell.

The only thing that we had at our disposable was a mattress, a frame, and a spoon. Up high on the far wall was a bar-less window, a window from which we could have escaped through if there were a way to get to it.

"What is your suggestion, Watson?"

"We do have a spoon and it is a dirt floor, we could dig a tunnel under the cell wall."

"That is true, but we don't know how deep the wall is and we'd run the risk of being caught by Moriarty."

"We could try to use the frame and mattress as a ladder."

Holmes nodded, and we moved the mattress and frame under the window.

Tried as we might, we couldn't make it to the window. Holmes even tried to climb up my back, but the window was still just out of reach.

Finally, Holmes discovered our escape plan. Before long, we were pulling ourselves through the window and jumping on the ground outside of the cell.

How did we escape?

The Case of The Undead Husband

One summer afternoon Holmes and I were relaxing at home.

It had been a long week, but we had finally found some quiet time. I was writing in my journal when Holmes spoke.

"Say, Watson, I have a riddle for you."

I turned in my seat to look at him.

"Certainly, I could use a riddle."

"A woman shoots her husband, and then holds him under water for five minutes. A few moments later, she and her husband go out for dinner. How is that possible?"

"That's an interesting riddle indeed, but I believe I know the answer."

How could this have happened?

The Case of The Lonely Man

Holmes and I stepped up to a small cottage on a deserted street.

We had received word that the old, wealthy man living at the cottage had been murdered. The mailman had discovered him early this Thursday morning.

Holmes spoke with one of the officers and the mailman before coming back over to me.

"The man was partially handicapped, so everything was delivered to him," Holmes began.

He recounted everything that the other men had told him. When the mailman arrived this morning, he had noticed that the front door was ajar. He peeked in and saw the old man lying in a pool of blood.

Holmes and I walked towards the house and inspected the front porch. On the porch were unopened mail, flyers, a catalog, Monday's newspaper, and two bottles of warm milk.

Inside, the pool of the blood was dried.

Holmes knelt next to the body and looked up, "I know who murdered this man."

Who is the murderer and why?

The Case of The Baggy Suit

I stood at the corner of Baker Street with Holmes.

The sun beat down high above us as the police secured the crime scene.

The main suspect stood off to the side.

After questioning some of the witnesses, the police had figured out that the suspect has brown hair, blue eyes, and wore a baggy suit.

The victim had been shot in the stomach.

Our suspect, Sean Baker, fit the description perfectly.

He denied that he had anything to do with the murder.

Holmes and I stepped over to Sean to questions him.

"Mr. Baker, please tell us what happened. From the beginning," Holmes stated.

"Certainly, I was across the street there when I notice this man walking up the street. Out of nowhere, a man came up behind him and shot him. I ran away as fast as I could."

"Can you describe what he looks like?" I asked.

"He had a red mustache and hair and wore a baggy suit."

"He's lying," Holmes exclaimed.

How does Sherlock know the man is lying?

The Case of The Sunday Murder

Early Sunday morning a bang rattled the door, shaking me awake.

I shuffled to the door.

Holmes had barely stuck his head out of his room. I opened the door to find a Scotland Yard officer waiting.

"What can I help you with?" I asked.

"Mr. Holmes and your presence are requested at a murder."

"We'll be right there."

I stepped to Holmes' room and knocked.

"I am on my way."

Once we were dressed, we followed the officer to the murder scene.

A woman sat on the porch, tears streaming down her face.

"This is the wife of the victim. She found him this morning," the officer said.

"Ma'am, can you tell me what were you doing at the time of the murder?" Holmes asked.

"I was still sleeping. I woke up and found him in his study. I immediately notified the police. That is all that has happened this morning."

"Who are these three?" I asked, turning to the others standing on the porch.

"The cook, gardener, and maid," the officer replied.

"You three tell me what you were doing at the time of the murder," Holmes demanded.

"I was cooking breakfast," the cook stated.

"I was gathering vegetables for the cook," the gardener said.

"I was getting the mail," the maid replied.

Holmes turned to me, a shining glimmer in his eye. He knew who the killer was, but I did as well.

Who is the killer?

The Case of The Misplaced Wedding

One lazy Sunday evening, Holmes and I rested in the sitting room when all of a sudden Holmes turned to me, a glint in his eye.

That meant he had thought up a riddle.

"Watson, I have a riddle for you."

"Alright."

"Five weddings were scheduled to take place on the same day. The newspaper reported the marriages but in a code of sorts.

The newspaper read: Either Clair or Dorothy became Mrs. Harley.

Joseph's name is either Farley or Darling; Primrose was either Miss Wicks or Miss Carlisle.

Either Sara or Miss Carlisle married Reuben Marley; neither of them became Mrs. Darling.

Marilyn was either Miss Wicks or Miss Read, and she married neither John nor Mr. Darling.

Neither Clyde nor Theodore is Mr. Barley, who married either Primrose or Marilyn.

Theodore was married to either Miss Hicks or Miss Carlisle; Clair was either Joseph's bride or Miss Read.

Miss Nix married either Reuben or John.

Dorothy married neither Joseph nor Clyde; her maiden name was either Read or Carlisle.

What are the brides and grooms' first and last names, and who did they marry?

The Case of The Mysterious Murderer

Holmes and I walked into in the kitchen where the body and evidence laid.

The husband stood staring at his wife's body on the floor.

Stepping up to the man, I reached out my hand to shake his.

"Can you tell us what happened?" I asked.

"Yes, sir. When I came home, I went to hang up my coat when I heard my wife shout, 'No John! Don't do it!' I then heard a shot and came in here to find my wife here, the gun on the ground and these three in here."

In the room stood a police officer, a nurse, and a maid.

"What is your name?" Holmes asked.

"Peter."

Holmes stepped over to the three suspects and looked them over before announcing, "I know who the killer is."

Who is the killer and why?

The Case of the Poisoned Tea

It was a cold wintery day as Holmes and I sat in the parlor of our abode.

Holmes was slumped in his favorite chair looking out the window at the newly fallen snow.

It was too cold to go out for any entertainment and I was tired of watching Holmes watch the snow.

I stood up and began pacing the room trying to find something to replace my boredom when a knock at the door startled me.

I looked at Holmes waiting for him to answer the knock.

"Holmes, would you like for me to answer the door?"

Holmes never moved from his chair. He lifted his hand and waved.

"I suppose it must be important if someone has come out in this dreadful weather."

I walked to the door and opened it. To my surprise, there stood a small ragamuffin shivering in the cold. Her face was streaked with tears and I wondered to myself how she wasn't frozen solid.

"Please come in, little one. You must be freezing. Come stand in front of the fire to warm yourself."

She sniffled and nodded. I led her to the fire and brought a chair for her to sit in. I handed her my handkerchief to clean her face.

"Would you like a cup of tea?"

She looked like I had asked her to drink lambswool. Her little body began shaking more violently.

I hunkered down beside her and wrapped my arms around her tiny frame.

"Please, little one. What have I said to upset you?"

She looked up at me with beautiful blue eyes that were pleading me to help.

Holmes had by now turned his seat to face us. He was sitting in his normal thinking pose. His elbows were placed on the arms of the chair. His fingers were steepled together and his thumbs were resting on his chin. His eyes were closed waiting for the ragamuffin to tell us her story.

She took my handkerchief, wiped her tears, and blew her nose. She took a deep racking breath and proceeded to tell us why she had ventured out on this wintry day.

"I don't mean to disturb you Mr. Holmes, Dr. Watson but my mum has been killed."

"Killed? How?"

"We were out of coal and food and it was getting very cold in our house. My mum decided to try the neighbor's house to see if we could borrow enough to get us by until papa got paid and bought us some provisions on Friday. Our closest neighbor is Mrs. Gladstone and she lives one mile from us. By the time we got there, we were very cold and thirsty. Mrs. Gladstone invited us in and rang for some tea to be brought into the sitting room. My mum added sugar and cream to hers like she always did. I only added cream to mine. Mrs. Gladstone also added cream and sugar to hers. Mrs. Gladstone didn't drink any of hers and I sipped my tea slowly. All of a sudden, my mum grabs her throat and falls over dead. I don't know how or why but someone killed my mum. I don't understand if the tea was poisoned how I survived."

How did her mother get killed?

The Case of the Killer Pill

It was early morning when a knock came on the door. I stumbled out of bed, grabbed my dressing gown and made my way to the door.

As I closed the bedroom door, I heard Holmes snore out and roll over. The way this man could sleep through anything always amazed me.

I opened the door to find one of Scotland Yard's finest.

"Good morning sir. I hate to bother you this early, but we need to see you down at the station."

I smiled at him as I was positive he was looking for Holmes and not me.

"I don't think you are looking for me, good sir. I think you are looking for my good friend Sherlock Holmes."

The officer was slightly taken aback, "Pardon me, good sir, but is Mr. Holmes in?"

"Yes, he's still sleeping. Let me wake him."

I invited the officer into the room while I went to wake up Holmes.

To my surprise, Holmes was up and dressed. "Oh, Holmes, you are up."

"Yes, why wouldn't I be? My question, dear Watson is why aren't you?"

"Me?"

"Yes, we have Scotland Yard waiting for us and you aren't even dressed."

"Holmes, I got out of bed to answer the door. I haven't had time to get dressed. If you will give me a few minutes, I will be dressed and ready to go."

"Very good, Watson. We'll be waiting for you."

Holmes walked out of the bedroom and I turned to put my clothes on. I could hear muffled voices while buttoning my shoes.

I grabbed my overcoat and walked into the outer room.

Holmes and the officer were standing in front of the fire chatting. Holmes turned to me and asked if I was ready to put my brain to work.

"I haven't had any coffee yet, Holmes. I don't think my brain can take anything just yet."

"Ah, well, my dear Watson. Let's listen to what the officer has to say, and I don't think we will need to go down to Scotland Yard after all."

Holmes turned toward the officer and motioned for him to sit down.

"But, sirs, I was told to bring you down to the station. We really don't have time for this."

"Nonsense, good sir. I'm sure I will be able to find a solution by the end of your tale."

The officer shrugged his shoulders. "Okay, we arrested a gentleman a couple days ago for killing his roommate. The only problem is we can't find any conclusive evidence. He told us a tale which made no sense to us but since you are highly skilled in figuring out riddles, my superiors wanted me to see what you could make of his tale."

Holmes nodded. "I see. Let's hear the tale."

The officer nodded. "The gentleman began by saying a killer will play games with his victim before he kills them. He will offer them two different pills and then ask them to pick one. One pill will cause them to die, the other won't. There is no way of telling which one is the poisoned one. Once the victim picks the pill and takes it with a cup of water, the killer then swallows the other pill. He doesn't die."

How did the killer survive?

The Case of the Mysterious Windows

Holmes and I were out walking one spring morning when we noticed a crowd of people gathering around the outside of a four-story inn.

We made our way to the front of the crowd and noticed a man's body lying on the ground outside. It is clear that he fell out of one of the windows.

I turned to Holmes.

"What do you think, Holmes?"

Holmes walked around for a little while looking from the ground to the windows.

"Has anyone been in any of those rooms since this happened?"

A housekeeper stepped forward. "I've been on duty since four a.m., sir. To my knowledge, nobody has entered or left any of those rooms."

Sherlock nodded. "Is the manager in yet?"

"Yes, sir, if you follow me, I'll take you to him."

Holmes and I followed the lady inside to the manager's office. She knocked on the door before entering.

Behind the desk sat a pudgy man wearing horn-rimmed glasses. Sherlock walked forward and offered the man his hand.

"Good morning, sir, I am Sherlock Holmes, and this is my trusty companion, Dr. Watson. I was inquiring about the dead man outside and wanted to take a look at the rooms on that side of the building."

"Good to meet you Mr. Holmes, Dr. Watson. Come with me and I will show you to these rooms."

Holmes and I followed him to first room that faced the scene.

Holmes opened the window and tossed out a coin that fell near close to the body. He then asked to go to the room above.

Again, he walked to the window and tossed out a coin. This went on until we got to the last room.

He turned to the manager.

"Have someone contact the police. This man did not commit suicide. He was murdered."

What did Sherlock Holmes figure out?

The Case of the Hidden Clues

Holmes and I were just finishing up the supper that Mrs. Hudson has prepared for us when there was a knock on the door.

Thinking it was Mrs. Hudson coming to claim the dishes we both voiced, "Come in."

To our surprise, there stood our friend Officer Connelly. He took his hat off and placed it under his arm.

"Sorry to disturb you good fellas but we have a murder that requires your skills."

"My supper hasn't had time to settle yet. Do we absolutely have to go?"

"I'm afraid so, Sherlock. This murderer is very tricky."

"Well, then, Watson. Let us go with Officer Connelly and see if we can shed some light on this mystery."

I grabbed my hat off the table beside the door along with Holmes' and handed his to him.

When we got to the end of the hall, Mrs. Hudson was just leaving her apartment. "The dishes are still on the table. Thank you for supper."

She nodded toward us. "You are most welcome. Are you heading out to work a case so soon after eating?"

"Yes ma'am, I'm afraid it can't be helped," answered Officer Connelly.

"Well, then, don't stay out too late."

We all smiled as we left the building. Without the motherly Mrs. Hudson, we would starve. She does get a little overprotective at times, but she means well.

We get to the bottom of the stairs and there sat a paddy wagon waiting on us.

We all clambered inside, and the driver cracked the whip and off we went.

On the way to the crime scene, Holmes tried to get Officer Connelly to tell him something about what we were about to encounter.

"I'm sorry Sherlock, but I was told to come fetch you. I haven't been to the scene myself. It doesn't matter as we are here."

The paddy wagon pulled up outside a grand two-story house.

There were officers all over the grounds looking for clues of any kind.

Holmes and I stepped out of the wagon and made our way inside with Officer Connelly.

Another officer stepped to the side outside the sitting room.

We walked in and saw Mr. Carlton lying on his back having been stabbed through the heart. Holmes turned toward the other officer in the room.

"Where's the murder weapon?"

"We haven't found it. That's why we needed your help. We do have four suspects. They are the driver, the music teacher, the cook, and the nanny."

"Okay, do we have the freedom to look around?"

"Of, course."

Holmes and I began walking through the house.

As I was walking around the sitting room, I spotted a piece of paper on the piano.

It was a note. I handed it to Holmes.

Holmes had been looking around the sofa and presented me with a note.

We looked at each other and headed out into other rooms.

Holmes went toward the kitchen and I went to the bathroom.

I opened the linen closet and there, on top of the towels, was another note.

I went running toward the kitchen and almost collided with Holmes he had a note in his hand identical to the one I found.

We took our treasures back to the police officers and they immediately arrested the murderer.

Every note had the same message on them: "The clues are in the notes."

Who was the murderer?

The Case of the Bad Apple

It was a rainy summer day, one where neither Holmes nor I wanted to venture outside.

I was reading the newspaper when a story caught my eye.

The story was about a woman who had invited a good friend to have supper at her house.

She had made meatloaf and mashed potatoes but forgot to fix dessert. The only
thing she had to offer her friend for dessert was an apple and some whipped cream.

She sliced the apple down the middle, placed it in a bowl, and put some whipped cream on top.

She placed the other half into a bowl for herself along with the rest of the whipped cream.

They ate the apples in companionable silence. While the woman was clearing the dishes, her friend died mysteriously.

How did only one person die?

The Case of the Murdered Captain

Holmes and I were taking a stroll through the countryside enjoying each other's company and conversations.

We came to a beautiful meadow full of wildflowers and trees.

"Would you like to have our lunch here or did you want to go a bit farther, Holmes?"

Holmes looked around. "This will do fine."

We walked to the shade of an old oak tree and sat down. I laid out the picnic of ham sandwiches, pickles, and olives. He had also packed some macaroons for dessert along with some cold tea.

We ate our fill and Holmes laid on his back chewing on a blade of grass.

I pulled my journal from my bag and began writing some of Holmes' latest quests.

There were times that writing his quests, would bring back a memory from my own younger days.

This was one of those days.

I remembered a time when I was a soldier in Her Majesty's service. Our ship had been called to aid a Japanese ship.

I thought this would make for an interesting tale for Holmes as it was a mystery we had to solve back then.

"Holmes, are you sleeping?"

"No, Watson, merely watching the clouds scurry by. It is interesting seeing how many shapes you can see."

"Yes, I suppose you are right, Holmes. Would it bother you too much if I shared a tale from my military days? It was a mystery we had to solve at the time that you might find as interesting as I did at the time."

"Sure, Watson, go ahead. My brain could use some stimulation."

"We came alongside the Japanese ship that had sent out an emergency signal. Our Captain sent out a yell, "Permission to board?" This was met with stony silence. The Captain motioned for us to board and fan out to find who might have sent the signal. We soon found the Captain of the Japanese ship had been murdered in his cabin. We found a master-at-arms below deck holding four suspects. Each one had their own alibi for the time of the Captain's murder. The captain's wife had gone to her cabin due to being seasick. The housekeeper claimed she was fixing the flag that had been hung upside down. The engineer had been fixing the signal. The cook had been busy keeping the wine barrels in place. After hearing all the alibis, we arrested the murderer immediately."

"Can you tell me, Holmes, who was the murderer?"

The Case of the Jumbled Notes

Sherlock Holmes and I were called to the home of a "Lady of the Evening."

She had been shot in her bedroom and had been found by her handmaiden.

The handmaiden had run to the police and they had some suspects already in the parlor. Their names were: Ankit, Tarun, Harish, Manoj, and Manish.

The killer liked playing jokes and thought it would be funny to leave notes in various places throughout the house to see if anyone could figure out their "clues."

One officer found a note in the toilet room.

Another officer found another note in the art room.

Another note was found in the restroom.

An officer found a note in the underwater room.

The last note was found in a room marked "No Smoking."

Every one of the notes read the exact same thing: "The clues are the places where you found the notes." The mystery was that none of the officers could find any clues in any of the room where the notes were found.

It only took Holmes a matter of minutes to identify the killer.

Who killed the Lady of the Evening?

The Case of the Mixed-up Witnesses

Holmes and I were asked to sit in at a recent trial.

I was trying my best to keep up with who was testifying for the prosecutor and the defense.

The prosecutor, Mr. Peterman called five witnesses.

After he was finished, the defense attorney Ms. Atwell called her five witnesses.

I tried to write everything down as I saw it but became confused and know that I have gotten things all mixed up.

I was writing as fast as I possibly could when Holmes leaned over to me and asked, "What was the name of the second witness Peterman called? I do think I know them from somewhere."

I quickly looked back through my notes but had forgotten to write down their name.

I had written down a bunch of notes, but it would take some time to figure it all out.

"Holmes I must confess that I haven't taken the best notes, but you may look through them and see if you can figure out the name of the witness you think you know. Sorry, I guess I just got caught up in the trial and didn't pay attention all too well."

"My dear, Watson, let me see what you have but I am sure your notes are perfectly fine."

I handed Holmes my journal and he flipped through it.

"Yes, Watson, these are a bit jumbled but nothing that I won't be able to decipher. It looks like from your information, I can see that one woman has the first name of Diane. Someone has the last name of Anderson and someone is an accountant. It shouldn't be too hard to find the names of the ten witnesses along with their occupations and the correct order in which they were called to testify."

Here is the list of Watson's notes:
There was a mechanic that testified before McNeil, but he didn't testify just before. He also wasn't on the stand first.
Mr. Peterman called these people to the stand: the computer programmer, Ms. Olson, Mr. Ducklow, Mark, and Kathy.

John isn't a teacher.

Mark was called to testify before Betty but not just before.

Ms. Atwell called these people to the stand: the secretary, Mr. Simpson, Ms. Fuller, Sandra, and John.

The bank teller was called to testify before Zimmer but not right before.

Neither Kathy nor Mark is a pilot.

Anne was called to testify before Williams and after the pilot. She is a musician.

Mary was called to testify just before Miller, who was called before the author but not right before.

Ms. Atwell didn't call Betty or Glenn.

Frank was called to testify before a teacher who was called right before Ms. Fuller.

Thompson, who isn't Mary, was called to testify right before the dentist.

The computer programmer wasn't called to testify right before the secretary.

Can you figure out every person's first and last name along with their occupation? You also need to put them in order in which they were called to testify.

The Case of the Thwarted Highwayman

It was a cold and stormy night. Holmes and I were sitting around the fire, each lost to his own thoughts.

I was working on my journal and Holmes was reading the newspaper.

There was a bolt of lightning, followed by a rumble of thunder that shook the house.

This reminded me of the time I helped save my niece from an intruder by phone.

Elizabeth has been sitting at her study table. She was home all alone. It was a stormy and cold night. Her parents were on a flight to Australia for her grandmother's funeral.

She had begged to go with them, but she had an exam the next day that she absolutely couldn't miss.

The storm became more violent and the wind began to howl. The noise was making it super hard for her to concentrate on her studies.

She almost dozed off when she was alerted by a loud "THUD." She shook it off as a window being shut by the wind.

She once again went back to her studies when she heard footsteps.

She slowly emerged from her room and entered the sitting room when all of a sudden, she was grabbed from behind.

She tried to scream but it came out as a squeak since the intruder's arm was pressing against her throat.

She tried to loosen his grip, but it was useless.

"Give me your money!" snarled the intruder.

"I-I-I d-d-don't have any here! P-P-Please l-l-let me go!" Emily cried.

"You're lying to me!" screamed the intruder. He was getting extremely irritated. She felt him tighten the grip around her neck.

She didn't say anything for a few minutes hoping he would loosen his grip and she could escape.

All of a sudden, the phone rang which made them both jump.

"I have to answer the phone. If I don't, people will get suspicious since they know I am home." Amazingly to Elizabeth, her voice was very calm. Her intruder released his grip on her neck.

"Fine, NO funny business or you've had it!" growled the intruder.

Emily went to the phone keeping her back to her assailant.

She took a few deep breaths to calm herself. She picked up the phone.

"Hello, Liz! How's the studying going?" asked the caller.

"Hey, Abby. Thank you for the call. Hey, do you remember the notes I let you borrow last week for Science class? I need those back. It would help me out a lot. It's sort of an emergency, so could you bring them to me tomorrow. Please hurry and find the notes. I have to get back to studying now. Bye." Elizabeth ended the call and hung up the phone.

"Very good, said the intruder." He was slightly confused about the conversation.

"TELL ME WHERE THE MONEY IS!"

"Fine…it…it…is…in…my parents' room. It's down that hall, first room to the right, third drawer in the chest." said Elizabeth.

"TAKE ME!" he screamed.

She took a deep breath, swallowed hard, and said a quick novena.

She walked toward her parents' room in total silence very slowly.

She had just reached the room when she heard sirens.

The assailant froze where he stood.

He went to the closest window and looked out. He saw a police wagon approaching.

He opened the window and jumped out.

Elizabeth ran outside just in time to see the assailant being handcuffed and put into the wagon.

She saw me and ran into my waiting arms. I hugged her tight.

"Smart girl," said the officer.

How did the police find out about the intruder?

The Case of the Escaped Stalker

Holmes and I were on the way to the tobacconist to get Holmes' favorite tobacco when we spotted a familiar face creeping around Ms. Turner's house.

"Watson, did you see that man?"

"Yes, what about him?"

"Did you not recognize him?"

"No, should I have?"

"Yes, but that's not important. Come with me. Follow my lead."

Holmes went to the door of Ms. Turner's house and knocked. Ms. Turner opened the door.

"Hello, Ms. Turner. I think I saw Freddie run around the back of your house earlier. Are you okay? I know he is very deranged and I'm afraid he will try to get to you."

Ms. Turner replied, "I'm sure everything is going to be fine." Her voice quivered a bit like she was nervous.

"Would you like for me and Watson to come in and look around?"

"Oh, heaven's no. I'm fine."

"Okay if you say so. Please send me a note if you see anyone or anything suspicious. Why don't you send me a note later just to tell me you are fine?"

"I definitely will be doing that." Ms. Turner replied.

Holmes and I walked back to the house and within a few minutes, there was a ring at the door.

I opened the door and found a boy standing there with a note in his hand from Ms. Turner. The note read:

"This morning, I tried a fun new seating style for the kids during the morning assembly. I helped arrange them into rows of twenty-one. The kids didn't care, but I really loved it. I liked the second column the best."

I wasn't sure what this note meant so I handed it over to Holmes.

He remembered Ms. Turner loved codes and Holmes thought that maybe she was sending him a code.

Holmes took the note to the table and sat down. He was writing furiously when all of a sudden, he looked up at me and simply stated, "Elementary."

Can you figure out what she was trying to tell Holmes?

The Case of the Frozen Hermit

Holmes and I were enjoying a pot of tea one
afternoon.

Holmes was slumped in his favorite chair reading the
newspaper and I was adding an entry into my journal
about Holmes' latest quest.

I was just finishing up when Holmes bolted out of his
chair.

"Holmes, what has gotten into you?"

"Have you read the paper today, Watson?"

"Holmes, you know I haven't."

By this time, Holmes was pacing back and forth in
front of me.

He walked over to his tin of tobacco and filled his
pipe. He took the time to light it and began pacing
once again while puffing away on his pipe.

I knew something bad had happened to get him into
this state of agitation.

I had finally had enough of his pacing and mumbling
to himself.

I picked up the newspaper and read the headline:
Town's Richest Man Murdered Late Yesterday. I
turned to Holmes.

"Did you know the deceased?"

"No one really knew Mr. Hemsworth. He was reclusive and had lived alone since his wife died about five years ago. His children have been on their own for over 20 years. I need to go talk to the chief about this. Something about it is bugging me."

"Okay, if you think it is necessary."

We donned our hats and made our way to the police station.

There was a large crowd gathered outside and we had to elbow our way to the front door.

Upon entering, we heard the Chief's voice coming from his office.

Holmes introduced himself to the officer at the desk and asked to speak with the Chief.

He was immediately sent back to his office.

Holmes knocked on the door and opened it. Chief Putnam turned and looked at Holmes. He let out a large sigh.

"Don't people have anything else to do than to hang around the police station trying to find a story?"

"Probably, but this is the biggest thing that has happened in a very long time. Would you like my help in this matter?"

"If you think you can make sense of all this nonsense, please."

Chief Putnam led Holmes to an interrogation room. Inside there was Mr. Hemsworth's son, daughter, the mailman, and another officer.

Holmes and I talked for a while with Officer Jefferson. It didn't take us long to realize that Officer Jefferson was a bit of a nincompoop.

"Can you give me the facts about the case, Officer?"

"Sure, Mr. Hemsworth's body was found in the icebox after the mailman, Charles, alerted us this morning that he thought something was wrong. A frozen body would normally be good news, well, not GOOD news. May he rest in peace. I'm glad to finally have a great case to work on. I love my job."

"Go on Officer."

"You would think a frozen body would be a great help because it preserves the evidence and body. The problem is we haven't been able to find any evidence. It looks like he was hit in the head with a blunt object but there isn't anything else to go on. We went over his house and nothing seems to be out of place. The person who did this made sure they were very careful. We have interviewed everyone who had any contact with the deceased like his son Ron, his daughter Rachel, and Charles, the mailman."

"Can I talk to everyone?"

"If it's fine with the Chief, it's fine with me."

"Thank you, I'll start with Ron."

Holmes and I entered the interrogation room. Officer Jefferson led Rachel and Charles out.

"Hello, Ron, my name is Sherlock Holmes. I was asked to help find your father's murderer. Do you mind if I ask you some questions?"

"No, go ahead."

"Do you know of anybody who would want to kill your father?"

"My father is the richest man in the crazy town. Anybody might have had a motive to kill him. You don't think I killed him?" Ron looked annoyed and a bit angry. "I got along fine with my father. When I ate dinner with him last month, he told me he was proud of me for having my own business."

"Didn't he loan you the money to start that business?"

"Yes, but that doesn't mean it hasn't been rough."

"Did you visit him often?"

"Sure, every few weeks or so. It might have been about once a month. Maybe a couple times each year. I would have seen him more often, but he was a hermit. He never left his house and I was the one who made all the effort."

"Thank you, Ron. If you don't mind, send Rachel in, please?"

Rachel walks into the room and immediately begins wailing at the top of her lungs.

"I CAN'T BELIEVE MY DADDY'S DEAD! HE MEANT THE WORLD TO ME!"

According to the Officer's notes, she only cried while being interrogated.

"When did you see your father last?"

"Well, it has been a while. I called him last Saturday. He sounded fine. I know you think I have a motive since I stand to inherit a large amount of money, but Ron will get the same amount. Plus, Ron owes dad all that money he borrowed. Ron has a larger motive for killing him. I bet he did it, so he wouldn't have to pay back all that money."

I had remained quiet up until now. "Wow, you can feel the love in this family. It kind of chokes you up, doesn't it?"

Holmes smiled at me and nodded his head. "Let's see what the mailman can tell us."

"Hello, Mr. Holmes, Dr. Watson, I'm not sure I can tell you anything more than

what I have already told the police."

"That's fine, Charles, just tell us what you told them. There might be something there I can use."

Charles shrugged his shoulders. "Sure. Well, his mailbox would usually get full of mail because he didn't like to leave his house even to go to the mailbox. Every once in a while, he would get a larger parcel that wouldn't fit into his mailbox and I would take it to his door. Every time I would ring his bell, he would always answer the door. I know it isn't much but he didn't answer his door this morning and I just got a bad feeling that something bad had happened."

"Have you seen anything off lately? Any suspicious activities?"

"No, sorry."

Holmes and I went back to the Chief's office and Holmes sat down with a sigh.

"Nothing pops out at you either, Holmes?"

"No, Mr. Hemsworth was a hermit who didn't come into contact with anybody; there are no clues, a lot of motives, no witnesses, and an officer who is a complete nincompoop."

The Chief laughed. Holmes was pacing around the Chief's office when all of a sudden, he stopped. "Hang on one minute. Hand me that newspaper please, Chief."

Chief handed Holmes the paper. Holmes hadn't read very much of the article when he exclaimed, "I just read something extremely revealing. I have just solved this case."

The Chief looked at Holmes like he had gone completely crazy.

"You read the paper and solved the case?"

"Yep, I just need to talk to one other person."

Who alerted Holmes to look at them as the main suspect in this murder?

The Case of the Servant's Wish

Holmes and I were out walking about town each lost in their own thoughts.

We hadn't gone very far when Holmes broke the silence.

"Watson, would you like to hear a riddle today?"

"A riddle, sure."

"Listen carefully so you will be able to give me an answer."

"Always, dear friend."

"Very good. There was a time long ago in the village of Brockenhurst where Jake had served Philip for over 30 years. Philip became ill and was about to die. He called Jake to him one day and told Jake he would grant him one wish. It could be anything but only one. Philip allowed Jake one whole day to think of the wish.
Jake got excited and went to talk with his mother about the wish. Jake's mother had been blinded in an accident some time ago and she asked Jake to wish for her eyesight to be returned to her.

Jake then went to his wife and talked to her about the wish. She got excited and told him to ask for a son since they hadn't been able to have any children.
Jake then went to talk with his father about the wish. His father wanted to be rich and asked Jake to wish for lots of money.

Jake went to Philip the next day ready to ask for his wish. This wish would make sure that his wife, father, and mother all got what they wanted."

What did Jake ask of Philip?

The Case of the Funny Mirror

Holmes had been in one of his moods for days.

He hadn't eaten or slept for three days.

I was beyond worrying since being a doctor, I knew the human body couldn't last much longer without any sustenance.

I had asked Mrs. Hudson to prepare all of his favorite meals but not one of them had been touched.

He had just sat in his chair with his violin in his lap smoking his pipe.

I had given up all hope when the bell downstairs rang.

I heard Mrs. Hudson make her way to the door and then muffled voices coming back toward our door. It wasn't long before Mrs. Hudson knocked on our door.

I opened it to find Mrs. Hudson standing there with a lovely young school teacher.

"Dr. Watson, this is Miss Bigsley. Miss Bigsley, this is Dr. Watson. I hope they can help you with your problem."

With that Mrs. Hudson went back to her apartment leaving Miss Bigsley in my care.

"Miss Bigsley, what could we help you with?" I asked as I ushered her into the sitting room. She looked tentatively toward Holmes.

"Miss Bigsley, this is Sherlock Holmes. Holmes, we have a visitor. She has a problem that she wants us to help her with."

Holmes barely raised his hand.

"Is he okay?"

"Yes, he is fine. Now, let's get down to your problem."

"Oh, yes, you see, my students have become very unruly. They are constantly teasing and making fun of each other. I want to figure out something that will help them when they are in tears after being teased relentlessly. We are on break for a week and I would love to present them with a solution upon returning."
"I see. Have you tried to stop the teasing?"

"Dr. Watson, have you tried to stop boys from teasing little girls? Have you seen these ruffians running through the streets? It is all I can do to keep them from hurting other children. I just want something to help the girls with their self-esteem."

Holmes stood up and handed Miss Bigsley a piece of paper. He had written the following letters on the paper: I. Y. Q. Y. Q. R.

"Go stand in front of the mirror and say those letters. Keep repeating it until they make you smile."

Miss Bigsley did as Holmes asked her to. It wasn't long before she began to smile.

She turned toward Holmes. "Thank you, you have solved my problem."

How did those letters make her smile?

The Case of the Wise Son

I had just returned from a trip to the countryside.

I could hear Holmes playing his violin from the hallway. He only played when he was feeling melancholy.

I sighed and entered our apartment.

Holmes surprised me by speaking as soon as I opened the door. "Hello, Watson. I have a riddle for you."

"Might I put away my things before you fill my head with riddles?"

"No, let me tell you the riddle and you can ponder it while unpacking."

"Fine." I placed my bags on the floor and waited for his riddle to begin.

"An old man had three sons. He knew his days were numbered and wanted to see which son would inherit his property. He wanted to test them to see who was worthy. He told them to go to the market and purchase something that would be large enough to fill his bedroom but small enough to keep in their pocket. Whoever could do it will inherit everything he had. All the sons went to the market and each bought what they thought would fill their father's query. Each one came back with something different. The father called his sons to him from oldest to youngest. The oldest son came in and place pieces of cloth across the floor, but it wasn't enough to completely cover it. The second son place had but it only covered about half. The youngest son came in and showed his father what he had purchased. The father told him that he was the wisest and he would inherit his entire estate."

What did the son give to his father?

The Case of the Missing Gold

Holmes and I were called down to the bank early one morning.

The bank had been robbed right under the guard's noses.

It was plain to see that one of the guards had done it and there weren't that many suspects.

Everyone was positive that Jim Hinkley had done it, but his house has been searched and nothing had been found.

Holmes was looking around when the Captain came running into the room with a note that had been delivered.

"I just got a note from the robber."

Everybody gathered around the Captain to hear what it said.

"I can't believe how smug he is being, rubbing it in our faces."

The note read:
"Greetings, thou puny toad spotted coxcomb! I trust you understand you won't be able to catch a master thief such as I. The gold has been hidden a short fight away that was hard to do because of its weight. You won't ever be able to catch me."

There were officers who had been keeping Jim's house under watch.

One called and reported that Jim was heading toward the shipyard.

Every officer ran for the wagon.

Holmes and I stayed behind.

The Captain returned two hours later upset.

"We were able to apprehend Jim, but we still haven't been able to locate the gold. Without it, we can't build the case."

Holmes came forward. "I have the gold. It was easily found once I figured out the note."

What had Holmes figured out that the officer didn't?

The Case of the Broken Watch

The police had called Holmes and me down to a crime scene.

This is what we saw upon arriving: The police were inspecting the office inside and out.

Martha, Mr. Hart's secretary who had worked for him for ten years was standing outside. She was a nervous wreck.

Mr. Hart had been killed while sitting in his chair. The murderer had stabbed him through the back of his chair straight through his heart.

The office was a mess, but nothing was missing. There were some papers on his desk that had coffee stains on them. Mr. Hart didn't drink coffee. There weren't any coffee mugs in his office. There were some gloves on the floor.

Mary only had three appointments listed in her visitor's log: Harry Marks at 2:35, Joseph Colton at 3:10, and Louis Willaby at 3:45. Mary claims that Joseph is the only one who drank coffee out of a paper cup.

They found the coffee cup in Mary's wastebasket. She said Joseph entered Mr. Hart's office with the coffee.

He left it on her desk later and she threw it away.

The knife didn't have any fingerprints on it, but the paper cup was covered with Joseph's.

Mr. Hart's watch had been broken due to a fight and it showed the time of 3:50.
Holmes immediately told the Captain to arrest Mary.

How did he know Mary had killed her boss?

The Case of the Grimm Reaper

Holmes was in a riddle telling mood on Sunday afternoon and was getting frustrated because I had been able to solve all of them rather quickly without much thought.

He asked me the following riddle and I hate to admit it, but it was one I couldn't answer.

There was a man who had three children.

Once the children became adults and the father was old, the Grimm Reaper came to take the father.

The oldest son, who had become a lawyer begged the Grimm Reaper to allow his dad to live longer.

The Grimm Reaper agreed.

When it was time for the Grimm Reaper to come back, the second child who had become a doctor begged the Grimm Reaper to live a few more years.

The Grimm Reaper agreed once again.

Once again when it was time for the Grimm Reaper to come back, the third son begged the Grimm Reaper to allow his father to live until the candle wick had burned out and he pointed to the candle in the window.

The Grimm Reaper once again agreed. This son knew the Grimm Reaper would not be coming back.

How did this son know the Grimm Reaper wasn't going to come back?

The Case of the Surprise Ending

Holmes and I had attended a funeral to give support to our friend, Percy who had just lost his mom in a car accident.

He was feeling very down because within the last six months he had lost his job, his wife left him, the bank took his house, and now he was burying his mom.

After the services were over, a man came up to us and informed Percy that his mom had taken another loan out on her house.

Percy literally had nothing except this note Percy's mom had instructed this man to give to him.

The note read:
My dear only son,
Thhaenrge! Tmhoe Bnaecykiyarsd

Percy was perplexed and handed the note over to Holmes.

Holmes looked at it and smiled. He handed the note back to Percy.

"Well?" asked Percy.

"Elementary, dear Percy."

What did Holmes read in the note that Percy couldn't see?

(Bonus Case)

Shelley was at her wit's end.

Her father suddenly died and left her $100,000.

He left her a note as to where he had hidden the money. She hasn't been able to understand what it says.

She immediately came to Sherlock Holmes to see if he could solve her riddle.

"I have no idea what he was trying to tell me, Mr. Holmes. I need that money to help me survive. Could you please help me out?"

"Hand me the note, please."

Holmes took the note from Shelley and read it. It said:
Get 21 pieces of paper out of the desk.
There are 14 pictures hanging on the 4th-floor hallway.
Take 5 steps to the right.
Go up 18 steps.
Take 20 grapes out of the icebox.
There are 8 eagle statues, 5 of them have no wings.
Remember the 13 stories about the 1 pirate.
Once you've done that turn around 19 times.
Take 20 steps once you go outside.
Go to the 5th tree in the park.
There are 18 flowers planted around the 2nd fountain.
Lastly, you should see 5 cats and 4 dogs.

"None of that makes sense, Mr. Holmes," Shelley said, "I just can't understand it."

"Not to worry child," stated Holmes, "I know where your money is located."

How did Holmes know where the money was hidden?

(Answers for this case will be given in the next book.)

Answers

(Answers) The Case of the Smoking Gun

I looked back over my notes of the events that had transpired, stumped. I hadn't even gotten the name of the deceased. I knew Theodore could not be the murderer because his brother was the murderer.

Since the murderer had his leg amputated, there is no chance of him playing rugby. Thus, Frank could not have been the murderer. Joseph had only met Theodore, so he couldn't be the murderer. That left two men unaccounted for, Edward and Leopold. Leopold couldn't have grown up with Theodore. Edward was planning on teaching Joseph how to use the lithograph. Thus, it meant Edward was still alive.

Edward, Frank, and Theodore were three of the four men still living. Joseph was also alive since he was going to learn the lithograph. I turned to Sherlock.

"Edward killed Leopold," I stated.

"Good show," Sherlock shouted.

(Answers) The Case of the Mysterious Code

I started at the so-called code. 7B91011 meant nothing to me. I could feel Holmes staring at me, waiting for a brilliant answer. Alas, I couldn't figure out what it meant. I turned to Holmes, my eyes downcast.

"I am not sure what those numbers have to do with this murder," I said.

"Ah, but you have reached the first conclusion. They are all numbers."

"What do you mean?"

"This was written by Mr. Patel, in a hurry, in the last seconds of his life. The B, instead, should be an 8. Thus, we have the number 7891011. If you split the numbers up, you get, 7-8-9-10-11. The numbers refer to the months of the year, July, August, September, October, and November."

Holmes paused, waiting for me to reach a solution. I thought about it for a moment. In a trice, the solution came to mind.

"The first letter of each word spells the name," I announced.

"Precisely. Thus, the killer is J-A-S-O-N, the secretary."

(Answers) The Case of the Card Game

I knew I had not stumped Holmes. He was too astute for this little trick, and he was quick to tell me so.

"My dear Watson, the answer is quite simple. To maintain a difference of eight between the first and third card, and remember that there are no Aces, the first and third would have to be two and ten or ten and two. But, remembering the first hint, I know the first card has to be two and the third would be ten. In the same manner, the last hint says the second and fourth card has a difference of seven. Thus, the second card has to be three and the fourth card, ten. That means the cards are two, three, ten, and ten."

He reached over to the cards and turned them over.

The cards revealed that Holmes was correct.

(Answers) The Case of the Invisible Blade

Holmes stood, holding the man's pants and belt.

"He was killed long ago," Holmes stated.

"How could that be? He was only found a few hours ago, and they deduced he had only been killed earlier in the day." I stated.

"He didn't die when he was injured. It only hit him when he reached his room. The killer, in an expert manner, inserted an extremely thin and fine blade in the belt of this man. Since the blade was so fine, the guy didn't notice it. When he came home and began changing his clothes, the knife that was in him came out, stuck to the belt. The knife finely cut him on the insides. That is why there is so much blood, and the incision was so thin, it was not visible to the naked eye."

Holmes carefully pulled the blade out of the belt.

Holding it up, it was easy to see that the blade was so thin that it seemingly disappeared.

(Answers) The Case of the Killer Puzzle

In all of the years with Holmes, this had been the quickest I had reached a solution.

The victim had managed to scribble out clues to her killer before she died.

"Please share your conclusion, Watson," Holmes said.

"In the message, the 2nd of January refers to the second letter of the word January, A. The same is true for the rest of the code. Thus, the 3rd of July is L, 4th of April is I, 2nd of October is C, and the 4th of December is E. Thus, the killer is Alice."

"Superb deductive reason, my dear Watson."

(Answers) The Case of the Club Repairs

I crossed the room and reached for some paper and a pen. This was indeed a conundrum.

On the paper, I wrote an x to represent the number of the original members. On the other side, I wrote $2040. Next to x, I wrote a y for the amount that each of the members had to pay.

Thus far I had figured that xy=2040.

Since four of their members resigned and left the remaining members to pay $17 more, my equation grew to (x-4) (y+17) = 2040.

To figure the total amount unpaid by the four resigned members, I multiplied the four and 17 to discover 68.

This brought my equation to xy+17x-4y-68 = xy. Simplified, it would be 17x-4y = 68.

Continuing to work out my equation:
17x-4(2040/x) = 68
17x^2-8160 = 68x
17x^2-68x = 8160
17(x^2-4x) = 8160
x^2-4x = 480

Finding the two factors of 480 who's sum equals four. The two factors of x are 24 and 20.

"I have figured out how many original members your club had."

"And?"

"24 original members."

(Answers) The Case of the Mysterious Hanging

"Holmes, if you don't mind, I think I have solved this one," I declared.

"You have the floor."

"As you can see, the floor is covered in water, yet there is no way for water to have entered this room. You stated that her neighbor had not seen her in a week, leaving you to assume that is about how long she has been dead. As puzzling as it may seem, the woman used ice slabs as steps to reach the rope. During the week she was missing, the ice melted leaving behind this puddle."

The officer looked at Holmes.

"Is that your conclusion?"

"It is."

(Answers) The Case of the Missing Sherlock

I stared at the list of numbers trying to deduce their meaning.

I turned the page in my hand and realized that the numbers resembled letters when upside down.
As soon as I noticed the trick Holmes had used, the numbers soon became words.

On the page was written "Bill is boss. He sells oil."

Bill had kidnapped Holmes because he had figured out his secret.

(Answers) The Case of the Misdirected Snowball

"I don't understand. It doesn't tell you which boy broke your window."

"Yes, it does. Read the note out loud."

I took the note and read it to myself.

"No, no. Read it out loud."

"I don't know what difference that's going to make, but if you insist. 'Question mark Crimson. He broke your window.'"

I thought for a moment. Something sounded different when I read it, alas, I still didn't quite see what it was saying. Then, I realized what I was hearing.

"Mark Crimson."

"Yes, he broke my window."

(Answers) The Case of the Missing Animals

I thought about the three men's statements. Holmes didn't appreciate the time I was taking to answer his question.

"My dear Watson, it's a simple solution."

He continued by explaining, the first two men blamed Tim for stealing two animals. Both of them could not be telling the truth, but both can't be false because that would imply that Tim stole the cat.

Tim couldn't have stolen the hen because the person who stole the hen is telling the truth.

This would mean that Tim would have lied, and that contradicts what we know.

Knowing that Tim couldn't have stolen the hen or the cat, we know that he stole the dog.

We know the Tim stole the dog, making Robin's statement false and Steve's statement true.

This means that Steve told the hen and Robin stole the cat.

(Answers) The Case of the Horse Race

I thought about the information that Holmes has presented me with.

Park couldn't be first because he finished after Royal.

Peanuts, Dusky, and Classic didn't finish first either. That meant, Royal was the firs- place horse.

If Park finished before Peanuts, he also finished before Dusky and Classic. Thus, it meant Park came in second place.

Dusky and Classic came in after Peanuts, meaning Peanuts came in third. That would leave Dusky coming in fourth and Classic coming in fifth.

I looked up at Holmes and announced,
"From first to fifth, Royal, Park, Peanuts, Dusky, and Classic."

"Good show."

(Answers) The Case of the Kidnapping

"My dear Watson, take a look in the mirror and tell me what you see."

I stood and turned towards the mirror. I saw the note in Holmes' head reflected on the shiny surface.

In the backward direction of the mirror, the numbers began to take on the appearance of letters.

"Why, it says Joe Jones."

"Yes, Watson, we know who Moriarty is going after next."

(Answers) The Case of the Meeting Place

I stared at the list of letters. Holmes favorite codes raced through my mind.

The numbers could mean anything, but it looked familiar to a message he had sent me before.

The numbers corresponded with the different letters of the alphabet.

Take a pen off the writing desk; I began to jot down the letters. Once I had finished deciphering the note, I left the flat and walked down to Enigma Baker Street where Holmes wanted me to meet him.

(Answers) The Case of the Frosted Window

"It's really quite simple," Holmes began.

He stepped closer to the window and beckoned for the rest of us to join him.

"The office had to be warm considering a fire had been built in the room, meaning the room would be warm. Officer, was there indeed a window wiped clear of condensation?"

"No, we thought the window had re-frosted before we arrived."

"I see. What causes this frost or condensation to form is the difference in temperature on either side of the window. The office would have been warm because of the fire she had, and the other side of the window would have been cold. Wilfred, if you had wiped off a window, you would have been inside the office. Thus, you were the killer."

Holmes ran a hand across the window to demonstrate what he had said.

Wilfred sighed and stared at the ground as the officer led him out of the flat.

(Answers) The Case of the Missing Birthday

I sat quietly, studying the snowflakes as they fell, trying to figure out Holmes clues.

Why he couldn't say his birth date was another mystery.

Today was January 1st, so two days ago would have been December 30th of last year.

If next year he will be 43, he must be turning 42 this year, so last year he turned 41.

If he was 40 on the 30th of December, he had to turn 41 on December 31st.

I looked over to Holmes who was still reading his book.

"Your birthday is December 31st," I stated.

"Now you know. Wasn't that more fun instead of me telling you?"

(Answers) The Case of the Two Thieves

I scoured my brain for any bit of information that would help me solve this problem.

I notice Holmes glance over at me for a moment and return to his work.

He must be testing me, but I wasn't certain that this would be a test I could pass.
"Holmes, you must explain this to me."

"Think about it, my dear Watson, they were two of a set."

Two of a set? I thought to myself.

Then it clicked.

Two of a set meant that they were triplets or of a higher multiple birth.

Something as simple as that has stumped me.

(Answers) The Case of the Missing Letters

"Would you please share with me the solution?" I asked.

I hated having to ask for help on this case, especially considering the reason I took it, but I wasn't going to be of any help if I didn't solve this clue.

Holmes handed the paper back at me and pointed at the first letter.
"If you look at the series of letters, you will notice that they are the first letter of every month; January, February, March, and so on. With that in mind, the last two letters would have to be N and D, for November and December."

(Answers) The Case of the Cricket Club

Holmes walked past the suspects as he began his diatribe.

"We know that the culprit has a wife named Mary. Mary is married to a man with black hair. Thus, the culprit must have black hair. The only suspect who has black hair and is married to a woman named Mary is John Alberts. John Alberts is the culprit."

(Answers) The Case of the Circular House

I turned to the mother who was visibly distraught.

The parents were innocent; they had been out all night. Alas, they felt at fault because they had allowed the murderer to tend to their children.

"Ma'am, you said the maid told you she was cleaning the corners, correct?" I asked

"Yes."

"Don't you find it the least bit peculiar that she was dusting the corners of a circular house?"

"I suppose you're right," the father said.

"My dear Watson, you were quick to figure this one out," Holmes declared.

"You mean…" the mother began.

"That's right, the maid is the killer."

(Answers) The Case of the Missing Child

"You know who kidnapped my son?" the Lady exclaimed.

"Yes, it's quite simple. All of your servants have real jobs except for one."

"What do you mean?"

"Surlamina, the Secretary of State took your child because she does not have a real job."

(Answers) The Case of the Secret Message

I knew Holmes had a penchant for alphabet codes. Certain letters of these words would need to be used to uncover Holmes' location.

The letters he chose to use is the mystery. I quickly jotted down the first and last letters of the words.

The letters I got were fsporrtesrkt rrpowk enzasrkt sryosrcsenbx.

Staring at the letters I realized Holmes' code.

He used the first letter of the first word, the last letter of the second word, and repeated throughout.

After eliminating the unneeded letters, I discovered Holmes was as Forest Row, East Sussex.

(Answers) The Case of the Killer First Day

"Today was the first day of school, right Watson?" Holmes asked

"Yes, it was."

"Then, one of these women is lying about what they were doing. Which one do you believe to be lying?"

"Of what they said, the only one that seems inconsistent with the first day of school would be Elizabeth's statement. She wouldn't be grading papers first thing on the first day of school."

"That is correct my dear Watson, Elizabeth is the killer."

(Answers) The Case of the Trapped Detectives

Holmes looked at the spoon he held in his hand. Pushing the frame and mattress out of the way, he began to dig in the dirt.

"I thought you said we couldn't tunnel out," I stated.

"We can't, but we can build a mountain."

Holmes and I took turns using the spoon to build up a mountain of dirt under the window.

Once it was tall enough, we climbed out the window.

(Answers) The Case of the Undead Husband

"Out with it then," Holmes exclaimed.

"Why, she took a picture of her husband and developed it."

"Ah, that one was too easy."

(Answers) The Case of the Lonely Man

Before asking Holmes to explain who he thought the killer was, I took a moment to think things through.

It was Thursday, and several days' worth of mail laid on the porch.

The blood was dried, suggesting he had been there for a while.

The bottles of milk suggested he hadn't taken in the milk in at least two days, assuming he received a bottle every day.

The last day the newspaper was delivered was on Monday.

"Holmes, I believe the newspaper deliverer killed him," I said.

"Indeed, he did. Otherwise, there would be a newspaper for every day this week."

(Answers) The Case of the Baggy Suit

"I am not lying," Sean declared.

"You are, and I can prove it. First off, you are the only person who has said the killer had red hair; everybody else said he had brown hair. But the main reason I know you're lying is that you said he ran up behind the victim. The victim was shot in the stomach. You are the killer."

(Answers) The Case of the Sunday Murder

One of the four people had been lying.

I knew that Holmes knew that, and I was certain the officer next to us knew it as well.

While no one could explicitly say that the wife was indeed still sleeping, or that the cook was cooking breakfast, or that the gardener was gathering vegetables. But I could explicitly say that the maid could not be gathering the mail.

"If I may," I began, "The maid is lying, and she is the killer. The mail is not delivered on Sundays."

(Answers) The Case of the Misplaced Wedding

I thought about the problem presented by my friend.

With paper and pen in hand, I worked out the solution to the problem.

After some time, I worked out that Theodore Harley married Dorothy Carlisle, Clyde Farley married Marilyn Read, Joseph Darling married Clair Hicks, John Barley married Primrose Wicks, and Reuben Marley married Sara Nix.

(Answers) The Case of the Mysterious Murderer

"How could you know?" Peter asked.

"You said your name is Peter, yet your wife screamed the name, John. The only other people in the room were an officer, a nurse, and maid. John is a man's name, so the police officer has to be the killer."

(Answers) The Case of the Poisoned Tea

Sherlock Holmes lowered his hands and stood up. He looked at me and asked me what I thought happened. I was perplexed, to say the least.

"Truthfully Holmes, it is a perplexing mystery indeed."

Holmes turned to face me. "Perplexing? Nonsense, Watson. It is elementary. This little ragamuffin's mother added cream and sugar to her tea and drank it all. While she only added cream to hers and sipped it slowly. Mrs. Gladstone added both cream and sugar didn't drink any of her tea. My dear Watson, the poison was in the sugar."

(Answers) The Case of the Killer Pill

Sherlock had been pacing while the officer had recanted his tale.

He had stopped in front of the window and was looking at the sun peeking above the horizon.

He turned to me and said: "Well, Watson, what do you think? How did this killer manage to survive while his victim died?"

"Holmes, I don't have the foggiest idea."

Sherlock turned toward the officer. "Sir, did anyone check the pills to see if they were actually poisoned?"

The officer looked shocked. "Well, no, sir. There is an autopsy being done."

"Good. I'm sure they will find that the pill the victim swallowed was nothing more than a placebo. Did anyone check the cup the deceased drank from for traces of poison?"

"No, sir."

"Then I suggest that you go back to the scene of the crime and find the cup, and have it tested for poison. It is my opinion that the killer poisoned the water and not the pills."

(Answers) The Case of the Mysterious Window

The manager looked incredulously at Holmes. "How do you know he was murdered?"

Holmes looked at me. "My dear, Dr. Watson, do you know the answer to this question?"

I smiled at Holmes. "Actually, I think I do know the answer to this one Holmes."

"Excellent, please enlighten us."

"If what the staff has said about nobody being in any of these rooms since this man died, then there should have been at least one window open in the upper room. Since any man can't close a window after jumping out of it, it leaves us to believe that somebody else pushed him out of the window and then closed it and left the room."

Holmes nodded in agreement. "Excellent deduction, Watson."

(Answers) The Case of the Hidden Clues

Holmes turned toward me and said, "Well, my dear, Watson, I was expecting something a bit more challenging. Wasn't you?"

"Yes, Holmes, it wasn't as challenging as they led us to believe."

"All the clues we found led to only one conclusion. Every note read: The clues are in the notes. Where other than the clues themselves can you find "notes"? The piano was the only choice. Once we looked in the piano where the "notes" are, we found the knife that was used to kill Mr. Carlton."

(Answers) The Case of the Bad Apple

I posed this question to Holmes: How did one woman die when they both ate the same exact food.

As in Holmes' fashion, he proceeded to say: "Elementary my dear Watson. When the hostess was cutting the apple in half, she placed poison on only one side of the knife. She presented the poisoned half of the apple to her friend while she ate the un-poisoned half herself."

(Answers) The Case of the Murdered Captain

Holmes had been lying there with his eyes shut as I recounted my tale.

I thought at first, he had fallen asleep during my storytelling which made me a bit mad.

I was just about to shout at him when he sat up and smiled at me.

"My dear Watson, this is so elementary a child could have figured this one out. It would have to have been the housekeeper. Why would she need to turn a flag over that is a white background with a red circle in the middle? The flag looks the same either way."

(Answers) The Case of the Jumbled Notes

Holmes looked at me and asked me if I had figured out the mystery killer.

I immediately told him that I had not.

He had me take the notes and look at them closer.

He made me look at them in the order of where they were found.

The light of realization came on inside my head.

"My dear Holmes, I do believe I have figured out our killer. It would have to be Tarun."

"Very good, Watson, how did you come about that conclusion?"

"If you take each room that the notes were found and look at the first letter of that room, they spell out the killer's name.

Toilet room - T
Art room - A
Restroom - R
Underwater room - U
No smoking room - N"

(Answers) The Case of the Mixed-up Witnesses

I sat and watched as Holmes wrote furiously on a blank sheet in my journal.

After only a few minutes he smiled and handed me the paper.

On it, he had written the list of ten witnesses in correct order along with their occupation.

1. Mark Thompson – Bank Teller
2. Kathy Anderson – Dentist
3. Betty Zimmer – Computer programmer
4. Glenn Ducklow – Pilot
5. Anne Olson – Musician
6. Mary Williams – Secretary
7. John Miller – Mechanic
8. Frank Simpson – Accountant
9. Sandra McNeil – Teacher
10. Diane Fuller – Author

(Answers) The Case of the Thwarted Highwayman

When I called to check on Elizabeth, she was smart enough to have muted part of the conversation by placing the receiver against her chest so all I heard were the words: "call...help...emergency...please hurt."

I sensed something bad was happening and called the police with her address.

The police went to Elizabeth's house at the right time to catch the intruder.

(Answers) The Case of the Escaped Stalker

Holmes handed me the piece of paper he had been writing on. He had rearranged the words so that there were in rows of only 21 letters.

He had capitalized the letters that were in the second column to find a secret message.

This is what it said:
"tHmorningitriedafun"
"nEwseatingstyleforthe"
"kIdsduringthemorninga"
"sSemblyihelpedarrange"
"tHemintorowsoftwentyo"
"nEthekidsdidntcarebut"
"iReallyloveditiliedt"
"hEsecondcolumnthebest"

Now I understood why she didn't invite Holmes and me inside.

(Answers) The Case of the Frozen Hermit

Holmes asked the Chief if he could talk with the reporter who wrote the newspaper article.

"Sure, we'll send for her now."

It wasn't long before Henry Gates was escorted into the interrogation room.

"Where have you gotten your information about this case?"

Henry frowned at Holmes. "I've gotten my information from the Chief. It hasn't been a lot."

"Okay, have you gotten any information from anybody else?"

"No, just what the Chief gave me. Why, is there more?"

"Absolutely, I have discovered the main suspect. Do you remember what your headline read? Town's Richest Man Murdered Late Yesterday."

"Right"

"How late?"

"Well…Oh…"

"Oh…indeed. The police haven't been able to determine a time of death since Mr. Hemsworth's body was so preserved by being placed in the icebox.

The police know that no one has had any contact with Mr. Hemsworth since last Saturday. The best estimate for the time of death was between Saturday and this morning when Charles alerted us to something being up. Somehow you figured out all on your own when Mr. Hemsworth was murdered. When I read the headline, I realized that either you or your source knew a lot more than somebody who is innocent should know. Now, you have let the cat out of the bag so to speak. You should really confess since this story has gone far enough already."

"Fine! Do you realize how hard it is to find a good story in this town? I was so sick of reporting on all the sniveling little petty thefts. It was driving me batty. I was dying to report on a real story. Then it hit me…I didn't have to be the one to DIE."

(Answers) The Case of the Servant's Wish

"Well, Holmes, it seems to me that there could only be one thing that Jake could have asked for."

"And what is that my good man?"
"The servant would have had to ask this question: My mother would like to see her grandson swinging on a swing made entirely of gold."

"Excellent, Watson."

(Answers) The Case of the Funny Mirror

Miss Bigsley left, and I was standing there feeling completely out of sorts.

"Holmes what did you write on that piece of paper?"

Holmes wrote down the same letters and instructed me to do the same thing. It took me some time to figure it out but soon a smile spread across my face.

Miss Bigsley's students would soon be telling themselves: "I like you like you are."

This was perfect grammar, but this would definitely help build the girls' self-esteem.

(Answers) The Case of the Wise Son

I went and put my things away while thinking about Holmes' riddle.

What could fill a whole room but still be small enough to fit into a pocket?

I was placing my things in a drawer when the answer hit me. I went back to Holmes with the answer.

"Holmes, I have the answer."

"Do tell, Watson."

"The youngest son showed his father a match. When he lit the match, it would fill the whole room with light, but it was small enough to be placed in his pocket."

"Excellent."

(Answers) The Case of the Hidden Gold

"While you guys were out capturing Jim, I figured out what the note meant. The "short flight" meant it was upstairs in his house. The difficulty because of their "weight" meant he had disguised them to look like weights. I found them upstairs in his workout room."

Since they had the gold, Jim confessed and another robbery had been solved.

(Answers) The Case of the Broken Watch

The Captain asked Holmes how he came to that conclusion after just looking over the crime scene for a few minutes.

"Elementary, Captain, first the watch couldn't have been broken in a fight. It was obvious there wasn't a fight since Mr. Hart was stabbed through the back of his chair. The broken watch was just a ruse."

"Okay, said the Captain. Anything else?"

"Yes, the coffee and mess were also a setup since there wasn't a fight and it would have been hard for Joseph to put on gloves to fight when he was holding a cup of coffee. The last piece of proof was the coffee cup only had one fingerprint on it. If Mary had thrown the cup away like she said she did, there would have been her fingerprints on the cup as well unless she had been wearing gloves."

(Answers) The Case of the Grimm Reaper

After I had thought about this case for several hours and still hadn't come up with the answer. I asked Holmes for the answer.

"My dear, Watson, after the third son made the agreement with the Grimm Reaper and the Grimm Reaper had left, the son went over to the candle and blew it out.

The agreement was "until the candle wick burns out" and not "until the candle burns out.

(Answers) The Case of the Surprise Ending

I had seen the note and had no idea what she was trying to tell Percy.

"Holmes, what does that say?"

"Simple, Watson. It reads: Hang in there! Money is in the backyard."

"How in the world did you get that?"

"If you look closely you will be able to see the word "hang" is inside the word "there." The words "money is" is inside the words "the backyard."

So, therefore, Percy's mom has hidden money in her backyard. My guess would be in the garden."

Conclusion

Thanks for making it through to the end of *Sherlock Puzzle Book (Volume 1)*. Let's hope it was informative and able to provide you with a few hours of excitement as you worked through the riddles.

The great thing about the books is that once you have worked through the cases, you can share them with friends. The fun never ends with these cases. You could even make a game out of it if you so choose to.

Answers to the bonus case will be revealed on the next book.

Finally, if you found this book useful in any way, a review on Amazon is always appreciated!

Mildred T. Walker

Made in the USA
Las Vegas, NV
03 January 2021